pappaji wrote poetry in a language i cannot read

poems by

rajinderpal s pal

TSAR
Toronto
1998

We acknowledge the support of the Canada Council for the Arts for our publishing program. We also acknowledge support from the Ontario Arts Council.

Cover art taken from *Sugundhian*, by B S Saqi (1957), artist unknown.

Canadian Cataloguing in Publication Data

Pal, Rajinderpal S.
   Pappaji wrote poetry in a language i cannot read

Poems.
ISBN 0-920661-74-2

I. Title.

PS8581.A486P36 1998   C811'.54   C98-932338-2
PR9199.2.P34P36 1998

Printed in Canada by Coach House Printing

TSAR Publications
P.O. Box 6996, Station A
Toronto, M5W 1X7   Canada

for Biji

Contents

The dead die and are gradually forgotten;
time does its healing and they fade.
SALMAN RUSHDIE, *Midnight's Children*

sugundhian; *the scents of flowers?*

i tell him it's me, your youngest
and still a quizzical look on his face.
i say my name slowly, raj-in-der-pal.
he mutters something about a child's red shoes.

saun ja kaka saun ja
lal plungh te saun ja
mommy daddy aunge
lal jutti liaunge.

a black and white photograph
enlarged to remember
pappaji *at a poetry recital.*
book in left hand
index finger of right hand pointed
and pointing
upwards or towards
the crowd—wah, wah—
or at the child in red shoes
"toon mainu duss.
how much poetry is there in your life?
enough to fill three books?"
(one posthumous).

welcome saqi,
just another glass
and i think i can write this.
just, just one more glass
and the right language
the correct form
will appear;
words will link
into ghazals, *into* geets *or* kavitas . . .

1

steer off the banga road
past the mustard fields and the gurudwaras,
past the sugar-cane harvesters
in the classic indian squat.
a rented ambassador.
looking for your brother
tara singh
son of late basant singh
in the village of herian
in the district of jullundar
in the state of punjab
(haalaat han bahut mare—militants and curfew).
looking for chachaji.
looking for you
in the greyness of chachaji's beard
the fold of his turban
the way his hands grasp a bottle
looking for your varicose veins in chachaji's ankles.

how much poetry
is there in tara singh's life?
when saqi-ji left for england
this big brotherly hand
that had gently held my head
and guided me
was gone.
for a week i did not notice
either sunrise or sunset.

        we must light a diwa.
        we must light a diwa and bless these ladoos.
        we must hand out blessed ladoos to the schoolchildren.
        pappaji would have done this if he were here.

to see your photograph on a mantelpiece
rotten with wood lice
in a house where i played as a child
and cannot remember.
pappaji

2

saqi-ji
poetry
memory . . .   i ran to grab your legs.
i'd never seen you before
and you pretended not to notice me.

your large hands
squeezed others in greeting the first time i saw you
squeezed a rubber ball i brought you in hospital
to strengthen your arms i was told.

pappaji *sits under the* nim *tree*
writes poetry
mother brings him his roti.
under the shade of the nim *tree*
no telephones ring
no motorcars motor.
under the punjabi *sun*
even the goats and the bullocks rest quietly.
there is only the sound of pencil on paper.
the air ripe with sugundhian—
the scents of flowers.

there are no nim *trees in alberta*
and sugundhian, *that's rare.*
so saqi *another glass please.*
i will write verse, make him proud.
saqi-o-saqi, *another glass please.*

pappaji
wrote poetry
in a language
i cannot read.
called himself saqi,
the wine server,
his muse,
left me in india
and sent me
red shoes.

3

pappaji *bounces a rubber ball off his forearm*
onto his biceps, into his hand.
an old army trick.
i used to count your medals
put them back safely
take them out
and count them again.
the other trick
was the one
where you made a blue pen
write red.

saqi-o-saqi,
the road to our village is careworn
and rough
chachaji's *bullock*
tied to the nim *tree.*
the branches are thin
and will not support me.

the poet's son stares at his hands
as they curl around a glass
(just two fingers of c.c.).
not jat sikh *hands;*
not the hands of a soldier
—lied about his age
and fought the japanese in burma;
not the hands of a schoolmaster
—the slap that disciplined an entire generation;
or the hands of a farmer
—the oxen plough and scythe.

nahin.
        not those types of hands.
sufficient to hold pencil and paper
or punch shapes on a keyboard.

4

mera juta hai japani,
yeh patloon ingalastani,
sir peh lal topi roosi,
phir vi dil hai hindostani

dil hai hindostani
and speaks in english.
when the poet and his son meet
words collapse in translation,
whole sentences change form.
can't replace "o"s with "oora"s,
"oora"s, with "o"s,
reduce thirty-five letters to a mere twenty-six,
say sugundhian *means the scents of flowers*
when it really means
the years apart
the poetry
the heart attacks
a child's hands pressing adult feet.

the poet and his son agree
that lal jutti *means red shoes*
and then settle for silence.

the dead cough when you laugh,
scuffle their feet when you would rather stay,
scratch pencil on paper when you would rather rest
than awake to fill screens with shapes.

the poet's son sits
computer terminal on line,
drinks canadian club on ice.
holds two wooden blocks
book ends, computer ends
bookcover stencils;
two halves of a face
the lines and the shade.

5

silver

silver

doesn't quite translate   you were never chaandi   *in my*
language sona *means gold   to understand   to swallow my*
culture   swallow me whole   leave no room for
uncertainty   left me with your taste still on the flat of my
tongue   the rhythm of bracelets you move over me
sona chaandi—chaandi sona   *bangles earrings*
sunglasses buckles on shoes / belts all silver
your mother and i accent   place a 'y' in poem
now punjabi pappaji *becomes fatherji*
sleepless nights when my hands traced your
back at four in the morning   translate gestures
to words   too used to being alone   you're not
here and i long for a cup of chai

secret

to a good cup of chai *is the rolling boil   steep   seep   swept*
up / away   memory shards   your heartbeat still
in my ear   pappaji *father* pappaji *father* pappaji
father   i became father became pappa
became   a flick of the tongue into ear   teeth
bites on flesh   missionary without a mission
just a position   best friend best dhost
separate and apart   now simply an entry in
your diary   the devil has read the kama sutra
kissed the back of your knee   traced the
hardness of spine   the hollow between
shoulder blades   suckled your earlobe
fingers entwine alternate   brown white—white
brown

6

hard

　　　to put on these shoes and not think of you   double
　　　buckled silver   arrive with paper bag
　　　borrowed shirt borrowed cds books   left me
　　　with your smell burrowed under my fingernails
　　　foreskin forewarned   for skin hard to the touch
　　　touch then smell your hand   under the nails
　　　and on the fingertips   trace shapes and words
　　　on backs   paisley thistle—thistle paisley
　　　p-y-a-r spells pyar   *d-i-l spells* dil   sone da
　　　suraj   *unbearably hollow   time and emotion*
　　　in a paper bag   time and a motion   take them
　　　back   no appetite when we met and no
　　　appetite when you left

hollow

chest   a place for you to rest your head   left me with
your breath still in my mouth   discard replace discard
replace discard replace   justify and box   sona *no one*
wears leaving like you   breast in rib cup   rib nest
tongue tied twisted like i never existed   everything
turned   the colour of eyes at breakfast table   grey blue
—blue grey   chaandi da chand   *reflective   hard*
cup breadcrumbs and think of you   add lachees *ground*
ginger   cinnamon   ground cloves and bring to a boil at
least three times   trace words in steam and bubbles
paani da pyar   *our time together   writing on water*

arouse

sitar
harmonium
hit tabla *skin*
flattened fingers of left hand
wrist-bone hardness of right hand
bend fingers to first knuckle
thumbs of both hands play a
part
mantra
raag
morning   afternoon   evening
rhythms spill into the space between
fingertip caress
earlobe
down spine
awake
erect

southall

that too-small
small distance between cities
herian *to* delhi *was centuries*
delhi *to* london *mere hours.*
oxcart evolution.
in this new land no processions
no celebrations of colour;
the streets a dull grey
every house a shade of brick
and a constant reminder of skin.

on the monochrome set
we learnt to differentiate
shades
white white to light dark to dark dark
tell randall from hopkirk
arsenal from liverpool
harry black and the monochrome tiger
i.s. johar *as the servant again.*
the black and white minstrel show
looked no different when colour arrived.

as you drove over the bridge into southall
a graffitied sign on a house
'welcome to little india'
nai zindagi nai jiwan
for half an hour every sunday
morning on BBC.

the winter sweaters offered no comfort
a dull ache in the bones
fingers over a radiator at school.
christian hymns at assembly
morning has broken in a fogmisthaze.
a child unable to comprehend
why the teachers

9

at fielding school
can't speak his language.

all these new things
the telephone
the bathtub
line-
o-lee-um.
at the greengrocers
the signs in angrezi
mind still punjabi
unable to translate vegetables
mistook a carrot
for a white radish.

angrezi *was a word*
not a language
something associated with chewing gum
and smart clothes
not the chime of angrezi *church bells*
on an angrezi *sunday morning.*

10

ellington road

francis walks his dog
at four every afternoon.
before the skinheads came to hounslow
he had a #2 buzz cut.
under his jeans
lace up doc martens.
when the skinheads came
he grew his hair spiked
and coloured it up.

from atwal's carry-out
on a saturday afternoon
at hounslow bus garage
punks on one side
skinheads on the other
ready for a rumble.
a word they all learnt from happy days
on 26" colour philips
in too-small front rooms.

this was enoch's blood river
gone wrong
for here were only whites
and now that tvs were colour
we saw the blood that poured
mixed with oil stains from buses
was the same colour as our inflictions.

when a turn to the left instead of right
could mean trouble
when a trip to the high street to buy shoes
ends in a chase through an alley.
when the son of the family
who owned a cornershop on kingsley
is killed
and the police won't say how

only they don't wish to cause community panic
his body bruised blue torn open.

the days
when field hockey sticks
were kept under beds.
trousers pulled over pyjamas
car engines started
the search begun.

one night gurmej
the next jasbir
beaten on their way home from the white bear.
jaspal with six year old kuljit
curls his body around his child
as doc martens and nailed-sticks
tear open
turn brown to blue.

the box room

from the box-room window
we could always see planes
lined up to land at heathrow
sometimes five or six.
the pear tree never produced much fruit
impatient we downed the pears too early.
in harvey's garden a pile of rubber balls
we'd kicked over.
after his wife died
he wouldn't return them
but when we were sure he was out
we crawled through the hedge.

pressing pappaji's feet
his legs
his final year
it seems he was always in bed.
pyjamas, slippers, a walking stick.
the roughness of old skin in a child's soft hands
the scent of mustard oil
purple marks on his ankles.

to bring you your morning
tea, egg in egg cup
had to sit the right way up
no tea could spill into saucer
a particular teaspoon
the diabetic sugar substitute.
the curtains drawn
the bed light on
your favourite parker pen
an exercise book open.

you left a pair of empty bedroom slippers
photograph albums
war medals

t s eliot—selected poems
g bernard shaw—st joan
tales of old russia—gorki, chekhov
mao's little red book.

you knew that there
was something you had to say but it was not until
much later that you found a way to begin.
ROBERT HILLES, *Cantos From a Small Room*

last sunday in april

on that last sunday in april
pappaji
knew his time was close.
closed his fingers
around any familiar
fingers
close by.

when prit *and* mohinder
told of another heart attack
everyone in a panic
arranging cars
to decide who went to the hospital
and who stayed home.
sukhi *with his head buried in the settee.*
the hospital   the bed of a dying man
being no place for children.

i walked from ellington to sunnycroft
paid mr. bhatti
for a new cricket bat
a practice rubber ball.
returned to the quietest home i'd ever known.

mourning.
the women in the back room
my mother wailing
supported by hari's *mom.*

15

prit *took me to the front room*
where men sat in silence.
a bottle of johnny walker red label
whisky tumblers on a coffee table.
a telegram was sent to tara singh *in* herian.

the next day ready for school
in yellow shirt
blue / green striped tie
and told that today
i wouldn't go.

all day
people came to visit—afsos
some i'd never seen before.
i sat on the swing
in the back garden.
the playground noise from alexandra school carried
over the alley
over train tracks
through our garden.

after the funeral
everyone talked
of how sandhu *made a fool of himself.*
bent over the casket
crying like a child.

there was no room left to park on ellington.
harvey commented
he'd never seen so many people
gathered for one funeral
and who was our father anyway?

expired sounds outdated

expired sounds outdated
we added the late
to your name over front door
as though you would be back home
sometime soon

saqi—black letters on gold
oversaw and controlled

the dead die
and stop changing forever
what would pappaji *have done in this situation?*
we still stumble over   over
try not to do what he wouldn't have
too little understanding
to know he would have changed
to surprise you with a drastic action
to move an entire family
from one country to another

wog to paki in an eight hour flight

fom wog to paki in an eight hour flight
from indian *to east* indian
i won the west in an air canada plane
with a landed immigrant form
during an oil boom
only i required a medical exam
and papers were signed

cold for the first time

cold for the first time
　　　　　again
that first winter was harsh
backs of hands rubbed together for warmth
frozen temples
schoolbag handle frozen by weight of books and fingers

all these new things
wool lined boots, toques and long underwear
plugged-in cars
curved shovels

sukhi found three kittens frozen solid
behind the front wheel of his pontiac
i placed the stiff corpses in a black garbage bag
set them on the sidewalk for the city to pick up

the kittens disappeared
nobody rang our doorbell
or phoned to say yes we've got them

they say forget history
and i've just started to remember.
KRISANTHA SRI BHAGGIYADATTA,
The 52nd State of Amnesia

collective amnesia

at a filling station
in a small prairie town
the attendant and i
practice a familiar routine

i answer calgary
he says no i mean what nationality
i say canadian
he says no where is your family from
you look indian

i remember being mistaken
native for east

history of the americas began in 1492
columbus mistook
took this backyard
for my backyard
carried on regardless

john wayne crossing the red river with his cattle
never had to answer to a native american
where do you come from?

the massacre more subtle
than blood covered midnight trains
in this country with collective amnesia

20

hollywood eyes
cowboys and indians
we don't talk of
tuberculosis smallpox or alcohol numb(ers)
we talk of two founding nations
and founding fathers
but nothing had been lost till they arrived

we talk of south africa
applaud the end of apartheid
and ignore the fact
the bantustans were modeled after our reservations

when children are taught a language different from their mothers
the old ways shed like baby teeth
scraped out like dirt under fingernails
that's the ultimate division
when one generation cannot communicate with the other
what unity then
what chance of resistance

the loss of language
the sentence of new words
the language at the back of the throat
throttled and silenced
the stories and wisdom of generations
not passed on   forgotten

doc martens are not indigenous to canada
they don't spring from the soil here
aren't formed in some lake
some prime / ordeal soup

> *in a bank line*
> *the bank of a canadian province*
> *that still has new in its name*
> *a teller unable to understand a coworker's accent*
> *says speak english*
> > *you're in canada now*

the language beneath the fingernails
in the corners of your eyes when you wake
wiped away by tip of little finger
how do i begin to explain
there is something i need to say
and i don't know how to say it
this new language has no words
for these ceremonies
for these spirits
for this land

 speak cree you're in canada now
 speak siouan
 speak salishan

let's make issues out of braids or turbans in the RCMP
canada doesn't have a long history
we must hold on to what we have
let's reduce time to five hundred years
for whose convenience
reduce everything to bilingual

 lisa's family has lived here since 1908
 her neighbour says
  you should have seen all the pakis in town
 lisa says but i'm a paki too
  no not you those other pakis
  fresh off the boat

driving west on richmond road
see snow peaked mountains
you want to keep driving
in the mountains
there you can really forget
half way up mount indefatigable
friends gone ahead
you sit on a rock
look at the lakes
and trees

22

it's so much harder to remember
than to forget
once forgotten
consider it gone

       a visiting doctor from kenya asks me
       where must i go to see real canadians?
       i've been here a month
       and haven't seen any
       and who was louise and why does she
       have a lake named after her?

i rename lakes and mountains
with a sweep of the hand

       outside the ship and anchor
       a young man in a suit stops me
          excuse me sir
          have you heard the word of christ?
       i say i'm in a hurry
          you don't look like you're from around here sir

to manu(scripture) your life
a wad of papers
in the bottom drawer of a desk
signed by a shaking hand
in a language not understood
even if we both spoke the same
i'm not sure you'd ever know
or ever try to understand

23

continents / new beginnings

रमेघव

the milk froze that year   kulwinder *placed a* dari *over leather motor bike
seat   rode with* kumble *wrapped around shoulders   stainless steel urns
also blanketed   were silenced for once   once   and* sukhi *still remembers
the first baby scream*

dI'sembe

*leather soles had no grip   high street sold out of hush puppies   lawrence
and i took a bus to richmond   leather soccer ball stung thighs   ready brek
central heating and conkers   mr sheffield wore a wool cap and mr roberts
grew a beard*

december

mr singh *in his sixty-first year cut his hair   shaved his beard   replaced his
turban with a toque   smiled scarfed woolen on the seventy-three circle
route   became in / visible overnight*

mishri *and* lachees

being two brown men
sat side by side
the flight attendant assumes
we're together

> *would your father like another drink?*
> *no, my father can no longer drink.*
> *then perhaps some coffee or some tea?*

being two brown men
sat side by side
vancouver to calgary
air canada
early evening business crowd
suit and tied
briefcased
i would like to know
what you do
and where you go

> *airplane light blinks seat 11D*
> *you read a letter*
> *that smells of* jasmine
> *a woman's face hidden by a* chuni
> *airplane becomes train becomes rail* guddhi
> *nothing was ever the same*
> *a secret shame*
> *that negates all authority*

in your briefcase
a mix of mishri *and* lachees
lachees *and* mishri
sweeten mouth
works better than mints or gum
from where have you come?

we exchange smiles
and don't talk
a gap like the bridge of a nose—
one eye cannot see the other

in your house
encased in thin glass
a small marble replica of the taj mahal
peacock feathers in a brass vase
a sitar *with broken strings*
an empty coke bottle beside your toilet—
those poor mis-fortunate left-handed

sons and daughters
unmarried unwilling
temper the caste
through marriage
and apologize on your death bed

being two brown men
sat side by side
count months of the year on knuckles
each segment of each finger for math
one language for home
and another
chuni-*veiled*
for outside
suit and tied
briefcased
i will marry for love
and have no shame

26

rungh

the colour of christ
after he died
while still alive
his skin glowed
black   brown   golden
thawa   miti   suraj
all basics like sandalsfishdonkey
(it doesn't look good, jaar, a white man riding a donkey
fetch the gentleman a motorcar
or a hathi
give him the cufflinks from your shirt
and a dark skinned man to betray him
or carry his cross to calvary—
sidney poitier, perhaps)

robert powell in the desert for forty days and forty nights
got so badly burned, he screamed
christ, give me more melanin!

> i always thought that canada
> was a white christian country eh
> till i went to winnipeg
> and saw all the pakis and the chinks you know
> not that there's anything wrong with that eh
> but i felt like a minority in my own country
> and i can remember a time
> when you could buy a headlight on eighth street
> those were the days eh you know
> now the gas guys don't even speak english
> probably never changed a headlight
> and get me another molson eh
> canadian of course

drunk he leaves the bar
gets into his big american car
with only one headlight—
a hand over his left eye
to stop him from seeing double

a recruitment programme in india *or china or the caribbean or* . . .

WANTED
LABOURERS TO CHANGE HEADLIGHTS
AT GAS STATIONS
IN SASKATOON
(EXPERIENCE PREFERRED)

the colonial christ
in margao *city in* goa
has missionary white skin
the dark skinned congregation
kneel at his feet
pray for better education for their children
a disease-free life
and that american jets refueling in bombay
make it back to complete their war mission

lazarus wasn't grateful
for his new life
death had turned his skin grey-white
it stayed that colour
people in his pind *called him*
donkey arse or leper skin
lazarus wasn't grateful
to be reborn a minority

there is no truth

1. *keegstra never happened*
   in fact jim keegstra was never born
   there is no truth
   only cinders

2. *as close as i can come*
   to auto / biography
   is my aunt's visit from london to herian
   angrezi *pantsuits and the sweet foreign texture*
   the first time i tasted chewing gum

   caught in a rainstorm
   only minutes from home
   i pissed in my trousers
   there was steam coming off my legs
   had to stand there long enough
   for the rain to wash out the smell

   in '76 a drought in england
   cricket *every day*
   fielding without a hat
   a scratchy feeling on the head
   the swirl behind eyes
   then everything turned black

   at nineteen a december chill
   mary's lips   mary's hands
   palm touching palm
   the finger lattice

3. *the closest*
   you could come
   to truth
   were words
   like difference

and culture
cauc / asian
pakis / tani
all these are my words
and aryan *too*

shantih, shantih, shantih
            T S ELIOT, *The Waste Land*

the heart of vilaith

didn't sleep well again
all night cats
knock over milk bottles

                    har yatra uthei hee kathum hundi hai
                        jithon o shuru hoie si

jaginder's *dad*
in his kodtha pyjama
kicks the pavement with toe
of english leather shoe
the pavement never gives
walks kingsley road
past houses semidetached
turns right at tiverton
follows tiverton around to denbeigh
then back onto kingsley
one arm swings to a rhythm
no one else hears

these houses have a history
if you'd care to ask
i'd tell you
harvey's wife died here
in their loft we found an RAF uniform
in the back garden of number 1
there's an airraid shelter
if you dig beneath the thorns
if you shovel till you hit concrete
our histories collide

31

in the garden of number 8
i once dug up a quarter anna
dated 1835
if you had time to not only drink chai
but to talk
to listen
i'd tell you

india had a history before
1600 A D
before the charter of the east india company
moguls and maharajahs
art and music
ancient caves and temples
the eternal and the ever-new
what made you think that there was no god here
what were you thinking
think what
shantih has a history
predates the waste land
if you'd cared to ask

in the fogmisthaze of london
people disappear
whole generations
in front of you hurrying away
sometimes footsteps echo
and you see no one
now shopfronts sprawl into street
sidewalks grow smaller every year
these roads not meant
for so many cars
the council solution
is to make them all one way
jaginder's dad walks his route
faster than you could drive it

a newlywed man on sunrise radio
declares a hunger strike

until his wife returns
he says i'm prepared to die
such drama
such thamasha
in the heart of vilaith
the news of the world
in the heart of vilaith
we'll quietly step over used johnnies
in lampton park
perhaps remark on the filth of the angrez

colonial
call on all
come in
want to clean toilets
sweep the railway terminus

and once the toilet is sparkling
the terminus dust free
then you must return home

oneupmanship
a lesson learned too well
to keep up with the gills and the sandhus
a race to the cornershop
a race to the bank to shop to house back to bank
through house a quick shop stop
back to house sleep open shop
wait . . .

for the bank to open

if only there was the illusion of shantih
the breeze blown in through an open window
predicts a monsoon cleansing
blows out the lantern
a droplet curves into the room
smudges ink
i will record peacock cries

33

and play them in my garden
i will fill my house with diwas
burn jasmine *incense*
if only there was time

walls that used to hide
now only disappoint
peaking over
just another
filthy english garden
nothing grows
sun never shines
faces grown angry darker
intolerant
they ruled us for years
now it's our turn
under the railway bridge
the graffiti no longer says
wogs go home
now it's safri *boys rule*

between the butcher slash video store
and the off-license slash video store
a lawn with white washed letters
spells
      jesus saves

there are shanty *towns in london*
in unused war shelters
underneath bridges
there are fires in rubbish bins
that never burn out

to cup an ounce of dirt
sift it through fingers
to say this is my land
this is where i will build my future
to cup an ounce of dirt into the corner of your kodtha
to squeeze it into a ball

34

and suck on it like a kulfi
i will take from this soil what i require
to say vilaith *is mine it owes me a cornershop*

share the same house
and speak different languages
no not speak but live
no not converse but emote
dil de bholi
english not angrezi

even if we both spoke the same language
i'm not sure that i could find the right words
or make them understood

caught in between
your children return home
by scaling drain pipes
lift bedroom windows
propped open by text books

35

have not come to terms with

have not come to terms with
the little divot under your nose
the smell of your hair
the way your fingers rest on fingernails
french manicured
catch candle
light another
you would think we could
communicate better
words in the right combination
to fill the silence
for three years we have sat
across tables
on sofas shoulder to shoulder
on barstools knee to knee
you'd think the words would come
you'd think i could just say
the little divot under your nose
the smell of your hair
french manicured nails
have not come to terms with

everything is old

everything is old
and love grows shota-shota
there is nothing i can say
that hasn't been said
that hasn't been said before
in the garden
the deck needs new paint
nails protrude
catch feet
the apple tree
trimmed in spring
will still produce
more fruit
than we could ever use

no kesh

no kesh

*a child with hair in ribbons   or a handkerchief over a bun   big brown
eyes and long curling eyelashes   everybody thinks he's a girl*

no kanga

later   hair spiked   coconut oil glisten reflects punjabi *sun   in a door-
way where you can't tell outside from inside   and what's the difference?*

no kachha

*brighton beach swimming trunks   tiger stripes   the english damp
goosebumps and shivers   crossed arms cover hollow chest*

no kara

*bare arms   that childhood bracelet grown too tight over adult hands
had to be hacksawed off*

no kirpan

*caught without a weapon   up against knuckledusters and chains   doc
marten imprints on* ranjit's *new shaven face   blood diluted by the eng-
lish rain   into the drain*

settle

get the job done . . .
three photographs arranged   too fat
on a table   too dark
choose either to spite you

     and i could use images that would leave you legless
     the whiskey tumbler tumbles through air towards a woman's face
     the fall backwards onto milk bottles—broken bones broken glass
     the choke holds   the open hand
     the unborn child in the womb—bruised

     a private letter opened by mistake
     the cup of chai gone cold
     ran out of flour for rotis

     a gold kara on your wrist
     bearded and turbaned for the day
     seven hundred pounds four haar and two coconuts

     eat and clean shit with the same hand
     filthy—immoral—disrespectful—unkind
     reject the breast that cradled
     when pakistani warplanes flew overhead

marlboro country

on the bus from colva beach to anjuna
he stands on the side of the road
cigarette in his left hand
a rifle in his right
a beautiful fair skinned girl lies on tiger skin at his feet
   fair hair   gauri gauri
   fair eyes   puthli puthli

catherine declares the marlboro man still lives in india

after kingfisher and banana-feni lit pancakes
the euro-tourists play a card game called cheat
the best liar wins
catherine and stephanie join in

two queens   —cheat
two kings   —cheat

the winner is the player who has no cards left to play
feni fumes wash down catherine's chin—evaporate
cigarette smoke obscures cheating eyes

in the bar backwall covered with pictures of samantha fox
the nepali bartender talks of sam on colva beach
  —wah wah unreal

sam on the delhi road
  —wah wah unreal

tall as a myth

       sam kabhi kabhi mere dil
       sam muje nind ney aie
        muje nind ney aie
        muje nind ney aie

catherine buys a pack of bidi cigarettes
plans not to smoke them

she walks naked across hotel room
flicks ashes
through bars in the window
cigarette burn
sun
    burn
salamander tan
marlboro man
tries to catch a salamander
the green tail comes off in catherine's hand

stephanie leaves catherine at all night beach disco party
where local boys practice latest euro dance moves
smoke dope drink rum
the bartenders tranced dance
donkey brays at four every morning to announce the time

early morning fire on arabian sea swells
stories of american allies
they know they will never see each other again
and feni fumes evaporate

salamander tan
marlboro man takes long slow drags on his cigarette
and puts matches out with bare fingers
on saturday afternoons attends the bullfights
actually water buffaloes
and not man vs bull but bull vs bull
horns sharpened with glass shards
the crowd scatters as buffalo decide
they would rather maim locals or tourists
than each other

shiva ram is a certified ear cleaner signed dr ram   —cheat

exchange travelers cheques with newspaper man
in sunglasses and topi   —cheat

buy genuine kashmiri *rug   very good price   —cheat*

long after stephanie and catherine leave colva *beach*
the hotel still smells of cigarettes
and the sheets still have sand in them

not many tourists this year on account of the marlboro man war

newspaper reports latest statistics
how many dead and how many missing on colva *beach*

under fishing boat night rest before early morning haul
tiny crabs surface where bodies fucked under fishing boats
where bodies imprint washable myths
one all elbows shoulder blades and buttocks
the other four-footed

across arabian sea kuwaiti oil wells blow legendary black clouds
into indian *ocean sky*
     —wah wah unreal

desert

the wind dries the lips
there is sand in every crack and fold of skin
static in the desert gives wendy wild morning hair
we've been here two days
on ends

once again the minority
the novelty
the only brown tourist
in the herd

musa khan *leads the trek*
wakes us with hot cup of chai
dulls the brisk morning

when we're alone musa *speaks* hindi
tells me his story
the son of the son of the son of . . .
a camel trekker
wants me to take his son to canada
dreams of his son as a bank teller

> *we have lived in the desert*
> *our skin turned to leather*
> *you can stick a nail through the soles of my feet*
> *and i will not feel*
> *will not bleed*

musa khan's *son recites the alphabet*
counts up to one hundred
names every well and every village on our way

we're so close to the border
that pakistani *fighter jets*
scream over us—
a streak of sound and vapour
disturbs the clear sky

43

there are eight of us in the group
five brits two americans and me—
musa khan *and his cousins have never seen a brown tourist before*
                    why would you come from canada to see this?
                    to sleep in the cold open?
                    to eat daal *with grit in it?*
they ask me the kind of house i live in
what kind of motor car?
will i marry a white girl?
they tell me dirty jokes in hindi
the punch line is always bamboo

musa khan *is always here for tourist season*
where the afternoons are too hot to ride we siesta
where there's always another limca salesman
over the next dune
when the season ends
musa *returns to his village*
where he has lived since he was born
when the days are the hottest
that's when you feel the crisp night cold

we lie under mounds of sheets
stare at the stars
wendy names the constellations
points with her finger and we follow
orion clear distant

44

herian 1

in the old house
with pink walls
blue windows / doors
i once opened an almari
found a scorpion
its tail held high
ready to sting
a snake behind a flour sack
a man with a stick
around which the snake coiled
older boys cut the tails off lizards
watched the green flesh wriggle
long after detachment

there was a procession
and money was thrown
there was a tinseled elephant
a white horse and groom
music and dancing
children on hands and knees
scrambled in the dirt for paisa

the opium addict amli
nomadic   alone
hands joined
in greeting   forgiveness
was asked to leave
          here we have nothing
          sirf roti *and* daal
          and a carbon copy letter
          money for this month has been delayed
the amli *said all the homes that were once his*
no longer made him welcome

by the boharh *tree*
a crowd gathered
to watch a cobra *fight a* mongoose

on another evening
when two brothers were fighting
talk of blood covered bu'shirts
talk of kirpans and scythes
talk of no man at home
sirf mother and children

> not allowed to leave the house
> and all i wanted was
> an india rubber ball
> to bounce off floor against wall
> then catch
> to pass the time
> when not allowed to leave the house

when pappaji returned
we had patakai at diwali
garlic clove shaped crackers
explode on impact
leave tiny black burns on the pink
foll chidian
flower birds sparkle in five year old hands
coca-cola bottle shaped candles
diwas all around the exterior wall
from our roof
herian aglow
when mother's hair started to grey
i suggested a trip to the city
there they can cure anything

curfew

when dakkus *came in the night*
pappu *sleeping on the roof*
picked up a clay water jug
smashed it hard against concrete
the sound like a shotgun
sent dakkus *back into darkness*

one evening after supper
the entire village lost electricity
pappu *and i with flashlights and knives*
tommy the dog by our side
walked to the generator
somebody had flicked the switch
we walked back in silence
to a room where three generations
huddled around a candle

the papers merely change the number
how many killed in previous night's battles
sometimes more military than militants
sometimes innocent outsiders
minding their own business
caught without
kara *or* kesh
searching pockets and bags
for passport proof

in chandigarh *the police took* raju *one night*
would have tortured him
if the DSP had not recognized him
as his uncle's nephew
trucking company trucks
rule the roads of punjab

people who go back now
talk of shantih *and freedom*

there are bullet holes in the golden temple
if you don't believe then just stick your finger in
feel the smooth dents swallow you

my mother's skin

my mother's skin
is old and cracked
tips of fingers
and soles of feet
dry and mapped

the sound of polyester catching
divots of dry skin

my mother's feet and hands
soak in mustard oil
her skin will become soft again
and when her polyester punjabi *suit*
moves around her
it will no longer make that sound

when father's father grew old
his legs no longer worked
and my mother had to carry him around
she would break bites of roti
soak them in daal *and feed them to him*
had to clean him too
still talks of the shit under her fingernails
and how that was her duty

i picture my mother washing her hands under a nulkah
first the right arm pumps and the left hand is cleaned
then the left arm pumps and the right hand is cleaned
mother can never put both hands under the nulkah
one arm must always pump

mani

when

hands on the keyboard are not your own
can't remember what you wrote yesterday
or were supposed to write today

when

every man in his seventies
has purple spots on his ankles
turban—just so
beard—just so
the fiftee   *the* salaie
the thathi   *and the* fixo
very particular
the family eyes / lashes

           you sleep chest down
           face twisted up
           an old man at the french doors
           is calling you
           wants to show you
           what once was will be
           a knotted finger
           beckons   whispers   recites

                    i have a strength that i wish i could give you
                    i have knowledge of the life i could give you

it's in the eyes lashes
the curve of upper lip
a beauty mark on the outside of left wrist

herian 2

the bicycle rickshaw driver tells me
it's mostly deserted now
mostly everyone in england
or canada
mostly those that aren't are trying
a country for the old and very young

as we approach herian
a child with a broken bicycle wheel and a stick
rolls past us
and announces to anyone he sees
that a stranger has arrived

there are some new houses
overseas money
oversees the construction
of new marble kotas
some have toilets
and one has a phone
no one sends telegrams anymore
no one ever comes back to stay
send money for the girls' high school
send money to relatives for weddings of daughters
new gurudwaras   hospitals

i am vilaithi babu
angrez in angrezi topi
hometown boy returned
the prodigal nephew
come back to reclaim
language and space

the old house seems
hardly a house at all
brick walls and brick divisions
on the roof a box room

ceiling collapsed
the pink of walls faded
the wood showing through blue
windows / doors
manure patties drying
against a wall

from the rooftop
on one side the fields
ready for harvest
on the other
the old houses
a horizon of broken bicycle wheels
hooked up as tv aerials

independence

in a rusted trunk in the back room
our old house in herian
i found your old documents
the first time my adult hands
had held your possessions

pappaji
there is a you i almost knew
and a you that others still talk of
and a you in these papers i'm trying to understand
the language mostly lost to me

a certificate of entry into the indian *army dated august 14th 1933*
on paper the day you entered your seventeenth year
did no one question the coincidence?

> *at the stroke of midnight*
> *the stroke of independence*
> *when boy becomes man*
> *when you leave the house of your birth for another*
> *when you're old enough to be a gunner*
> *when details like birthdates are overlooked*

i know nothing of war or fighting
only that those who were there
prefer not to talk

i know nothing of you
only that you preferred not to talk
of economic necessity
of lying about your age
i know that your father's name was basant singh
your mother's name is already lost to me

in a scrap book
in a child's handwriting

the story of the mountain and the squirrel
but the small things have made the world
a year is made up of days nights and weathers
i feel no disgrace
if i am not so large as you, you are not so small as i

pappaji
i'm amused by the thought
of you learning english
from karl marx and mao tse tung
in translation

there was that one time
you helped me with homework
not homework—i was too young
but something at school
i was having difficulty
understanding
maths, i think
we sat in the back garden
i wasn't on your knee
but near you
and not frightened
that was half an hour
all the more precious
the only half hour in ten years

the language of those years was already confused
one language for home and another for school
i remember the bindia chamkagi chudi shunkagi
the chal chal chal mera hathi, mera sathi
the chaaltha chaaltha *from* pakeezah
(impossible not to hear the train whistle)
no words that you spoke directly to me

fourteen years and a day after you joined the army
india *gained its independence*
at the stroke of midnight

when borders cut across railway tracks
through provinces
farmland
when neighbours became enemies

in your early twenties you were already fighting in a war
stationed in burma
winning medals for bravery

> *i was born too late*
> *by then*
> *you were in england*
> *busying yourself in work and politics*
> *catching red buses*
> *and keeping to timetables*
> *sending money and red shoes*
> *back to* india

the heriansouthallhounslow
of life
the places
we
were together
briefly

in that rusted trunk
a copy of an order
from the sikh gurudwaras *tribunal* lahore
dated 25th day of may 1935
the residents of herian-*listed in a petition*
*#47—*basant singh *son of* sahib singh
*#57—*basant singh *son of* dosondha singh
i'm not sure which basant singh *is your father*

i know nothing of the generations that preceded you
our history stops at a name in a petition
that lists residents as the sons of . . .
no mention of daughters or wives

54

in scrap books
the paper browned and aged
found unfinished poems
blue punjabi *and* urdu *words in fountain*
pen ink
lines crossed and rewritten
whole poems pencilled through
edges / remains of pages torn out
the lost language of those years

> *my early twenties were full*
> *of others' suicide*
> *attempts and depression*
> *still held back by the image*
> *of twenty-six antidepressants*
> *cupped into a palm*
> *one for each year*

> *had to leave to find my independence*
> *alone in an apartment*
> *after growing up in a house*
> *where three generations slept*

now i'm starting to become
the you i remember
nose eyes forehead
taking on your shapes
and the cut in the ear
forebodes
a similar end

wrapped in brown paper
tied with string
the book cover stencils
of your first book of poetry—sugundhian
the artist's original drawing
the face of a woman
flowers and dotted lines

55

apna sangeet

1.

wanted you in silver ankle bracelets, bhangra *dance to* apna sangeet
ours and hours alone on trains in buses in rickshaws *at* gurudwaras
where my gurus *left hoofed imprints and remnants of holy wars   cover
your head and remove your shoes, and when the* prashad *comes around cup
both hands like when you used to catch saskatchewan snow   understood the
message and not the language*

2.

heels hit hard dry ground as tablas *and* harmonium *play* bhangra *disco*
apna sangeet   *(silver left rashes on your skin and cut my legs to shreds)
white marble statue of classical* indian *dancing girl rhythm on my chest left
me bruised in places where no one could guess just how badly you kept
rhythm*

3.

red wine stains on an indian *rayon shirt that grew out of me paisley   you
wore outside-in   (the faded look like a tan in winter)   rye-on-the-rocks and
a vodka-and-soda, a squeeze of lime   alcoholic touches snatches in time in
places where no one could guess you in silver ankle bracelets dance* bhangra
to apna sangeet

4.

watched the sunset rajasthani *red on the* thar *desert   love poems that i
never showed you   wrote in broken english, spoke in broken* hindi, *thought
in broken gestures you never understood   not* apna sangeet *but our song
ours and hours alone   wanted you in black and gold silk* sari *with a red*
bindi *in middle of forehead   the third eye supposed to give your soul in /
sight*

5.

you broke into my travels   the sick, the poor, lame and blind hold out empty
cupped hands to strangers unable to speak their language and choosing to
ignore their gestures   at airports, in hotels in unfamiliar cities with
mosquitoes dance around your ear so you know they're there, and you don't
feel their bite till after they've gone

6.

and return to compare tans   but your hair lightened with sunlight   eyes
turned red from alcohol, repeat the old patterns   repeat broken circles
tanned through bicycle gloves   purple paisley on udaipur silk a simla
shawl wool gold and black blame the camera for the colour of eyes your
fingers loosen ribboned hair

7.

saskatchewan snow cold on your tongue   melt like words in your mouth
too hollow   translate one language to another   one word does not equal
another, one phrase not another   apna sangeet never our song   sajan o
sajan eyeslipsmouths in a darkened kitchen with shadows, paisley or maple
on the walls and the ceiling   your paisley eyes open, always open   dis-
tracted by a jingle   apna sangeet on the radio   silver ankle bracelets or
coins in a cup

8.

still smell your smell in my clothes   open door enter room to apna sangeet
on the radio   your cardamom breath your lips your silky universal
tongue tries to grasp my language concepts of the extended family arranged
marriages and a thirty-five letter alphabet   sounds never formed, chords
never used

9.

outdoor concerts at prince's island   broken drink glasses on patios on
summer afternoons   count ten fingers ten toes to the sound of ankle
bracelets   kiss decorated eyelids to the sound of ankle bracelets   make love
to the sound of ankle bracelets to apna sangeet on the radio   oh no i've
said too much   the sun no longer tans a golden circle on your finger   and
i haven't said enough

grow

       growing grown up and old   to watch the space around
       your eyes grow deep hollow   your rings loosen   fall
       hide in corners gather dust   your skin lose its reflective
       grow sallow   fingers grow knotted like ginger roots
       unable to twist the twist-off cap   your hair to thin
       clog up the bath drain   stomach not firm but folded
       body stooped over   grow small   grow small   and a
       love still raw after decades together   to cup your earlobe
       when the name in the papers   reads too much like one
       we think we used to know

kismet

sometimes two drops, sometimes three . . .

there are stories in the lives of others . . .
doosryan di zindagi vich kahanian hundian ney . . .
not dominoes,
you make the stops.

the baby—not her own
rests in my mother's hand
body centered on palm
head cupped between middle and index fingers
legs crossed over wrist
each inhale an effort
each exhale a relief
passes from her palm into her arm into . . .
with a straw made from dried grass
her other hand draws milk from a bowl
lets a drop fall onto the baby's lips
and disappear into the hardly body
another drop
then another
now instead the milk runs over lips
down chin
catches in the folds of the neck
every hour she does this

sometimes two drops, sometimes three . . .

i will never know.
mein kade nahin jaan sakda.

59

kismet *in a capulet*
a baby in a neighbouring pind *saved*
she has taken cotton from an old rajai
laid it in a shoebox
she will not sleep for longer than one hour
has no timepiece
and wakes every distance between herian *and* banga
a week later she returns jagjit *to his mother*
no words are spoken

kismet *in a sneeze*
  in an empty pair of shoes that point to an exit
  in mustard oil in a doorway into our house.

kismet *meant shit under fingernails*
    separation from sisters
    doli—*the journey from maiden to marital.*

i will never know stories in the lives of others.
mein doosryan di zindagi deeyan kahanian kade nahin jaan sakda.

and when they ask about kismet
what will you tell them;
sweets from jullundur
choodyan *from* amritsar
silk shawl from delhi
or alcoholic stupidity
he wanted to hit you and your children held him back
what will people say then.

i want to live others' stories.
mein doosryan deeyan kahanian jiwanyan chahunda haan.

yesterday the road was hot dry earth
today it is tarmac with a layer of snow
and tomorrow i will lose my eyesight.
not dominoes
you make the stops.
kismet *in the lungs of first child a daughter*

epilepsy and cataracts
widowhood—a bleach smell and a fiery oven
a frosted window seat—silence snowed in for days.

to understand other's lives
to know kismet *in the waters of the bow river*
with my four daughters.
doosryan deeyan zindagian samjhan laie
aapnyan char betian naal bow nadi
de paani vich kismet dekhni.

> *the old man couldn't bend down in time*
> *the piss ran down his leg*
> *his companion, a young girl*
> *granddaughter / great niece / guardian*
> *grabs the cloth of his* lungi
> *and wrings it dry*
> *the old man's hand rests on the girl's head*
> *no words are spoken*

kismet
kiss mouth
tongue parts teeth
why do you never speak?
speak to me.
talk of past lives—do you think we knew each other?
reading each other's horoscopes in different cities
becomes we were never meant to be
the permanence of lines on a hand.
a tongue stretches and tips a domino.
you make the stops.

i will never know the stories in other's lives.
i will never know the lives in other's stories.
mein doosryan di zindagi deeyan kahanian kade nahin jaan sakda.
mein doosryan deeyan kahanian vich zindagian kade nahin jaan
sakda.

61

outside the red cross in margao
an old woman
toothless in rags
puts her hand out for money
i tell her my story—
robbed on colva *beach*
her hand reaches up
and my head goes down to meet it
she walks away in silence

jagjit *does not know* jagjit's *story.*
bends down to touch my mother's feet
rolls hands back towards forehead
*joins them in greeting—*sat siri akal.
mother's hand blesses the top of jagjit's *head*
then the tops of his children's heads.

jagjit *does not know* jagjit's *story.*
jagjit jagjit di kahani nahin jaanda.

> *international arrivals at calgary airport*
> *flight from london delayed*
> *the old cliché-joke*
> *a dozen people there to greet one*
> *parents   uncles   aunties*
> *children   nephews   nieces*
> *passengers emerge*
> *an old man*
> *bearded turbaned thick spectacles*
> *beside him a frail old woman*
> *pink* salwar kamiz
> *faded* indian *cotton*

> *one by one*
> *the adults in the waiting group*
> *touch the feet of this couple*
> *raise hands to foreheads*
> *exchange* sat siri akals
> *embrace and move aside*

children are lifted to have faces kissed
                                    heads blessed
    the final embrace
    between two women
    their bodies shake
    heads rest against one shoulder
    then the other

close

and the day will come
when legs no longer work
bed / ridden
or always in a wheelchair
meri bamaar pursi noonh ek din aunge saqi
saqi *will come*
pour one final glass
thumb and index finger make a check mark
close eyelids

Acknowledgements

I would like to thank Fred Wah for giving me the courage to write about what really matters. Richard Harrison for helping to turn this into a manuscript.

The following writers are owed much for their inspiration, friendship and editorial comments: Phinder Dulai, Sadhu Binning, jbhohm, Roberta Rees, Shane Rhodes and Ashok Mathur.

Thank you to the collectives of both the desh pardesh Intra/National Arts Festival and filling Station magazine.

Some of these poems have appeared in the following periodicals: absinthe, filling Station, rungh, verb and Ariel.